From Zeus
to Aliens

Kirsten Anderson

STECK-VAUGHN
ELEMENTARY · SECONDARY · ADULT · LIBRARY

A Harcourt Company

www.steck-vaughn.com

Photography: Cover ©Darren Winter/CORBIS; p.iv ©Darren Winter/CORBIS; p.2 ©Mimmo Jodice/CORBIS; p.5 ©Digital Art/CORBIS; p.6 ©Sierra Studio; pp.8, 11, 13 ©Bettmann/CORBIS; pp.14, 16 ©Hulton Archive; p.24 ©Bettmann/CORBIS; p.27 ©Joseph Sohm/ChromoSohm, Inc./CORBIS; p.28 ©AP/Wide World Photos; p.32 ©Christopher Cormack/CORBIS; p.35 ©Pictor International/PictureQuest; p.36 ©Stockbyte/PictureQuest; p.40 ©Tim Fuller; p.53 ©CORBIS; p.55 ©Sierra Studio.

Art: pp. 6,19, 55 Todd Dakins; pp. 42, 45, 47, 50 Jeff Shelly.

ISBN 0-7398-5177-2

Printed in China.

2 3 4 5 6 7 8 9   LB   06 05 04 03

Contents

CHAPTER 1

Old Myths and Modern Monsters

One day when Earth was still young, something happened that almost ended the human race. While a girl named Persephone picked flowers in a field, danger lurked nearby. A king from a distant kingdom was watching the girl and fell in love with her. He **abducted** Persephone and took her to his kingdom.

The girl's mother, Demeter, had power over all the plants on Earth. When she learned that her daughter had been kidnapped, she threatened to destroy all of Earth's fruits and vegetables. The human race would die of **starvation** if Persephone were not returned to her.

◄ *Travelers from space are a modern idea.*

The most powerful being in this ancient world was Zeus. Zeus said he could free Persephone if she hadn't eaten any food in this other kingdom. Unfortunately, the girl had already tasted a bit of fruit.

Zeus could not free her, but he reached a **compromise** with the king. Persephone could come home for part of every year, but she had to live with the king for the rest of the year. Still angry, Demeter allowed crops to grow only while her daughter was at home. The rest of the year, all of Earth's plants produced no food.

The ancient Greeks told stories about Demeter.

Ancient Myths

Does this sound like an entertaining story? Ancient Greeks told tales such as this one for a different reason. Their stories explained what they saw in the world around them. The story about Demeter's daughter helped people understand the changing seasons. When Persephone **resided** with the king, nothing grew. When she came back home, plants burst into life.

Many tales in the ancient world explained natural **phenomena**. One tale explained the daily cycle of the sun and moon. In this story, Apollo and Artemis rode chariots that pulled the sun and moon across the sky. Another story told about a woman named Pandora whose curiosity tempted her to open a special box. When she did, she accidentally let evil and disease into the world.

For centuries, people believed these tales. The old tales are now called *myths*. Myths are stories that explain natural events, history, or special qualities in people.

Today's Myths

You might think we no longer need myths. After all, scientists now offer other explanations for the seasons, the movements of the sun and moon, and disease. Yet we are still creating new myths. Why? We use myths to help us explain the unknown and predict the future. As a society, we use myths to guide behavior. What kinds of myths do we create?

Monster Tales Imagine camping in the mountains and seeing a large, **humanoid** creature among the trees. It looks like a person but not exactly. You call it a monster. If you tell other people about it, they might look for the creature. They might even spot it or think they spot it. Soon everyone might be talking about the monster in the mountains.

UFO Sightings A **mystifying** light darts across the sky. Could it be a spaceship from another planet? If no one gives you a better explanation, you might believe it is. Then a man on television claims he was taken to another planet. He describes it in such detail that you feel as if you were there. ⚡

Superstitions A superstition is a belief that an event or an action can influence future events. Imagine finding an unusual button on the street and putting it in your pocket. If the day went really well, you might tell friends that the button brought you good luck. Your friends might start looking for lucky buttons, too. You've created a superstition!

What would you tell people if you saw this in the sky?

Urban Legends A friend tells you a really scary story. You're not sure it's true, but your friend insists it happened to a **trustworthy** friend of a friend. It must be true! Plus, it's a good story, so you tell other people. You've just helped pass on an **urban** legend.

How Do We Know?

People tell each other many stories and insist that they're true. How can you tell if they are true or not? The best way to decide is to listen to arguments for both sides of the story. Some explanations might sound silly at first, but try listening anyway. Once you've **weighed** both sides, you can decide on your own explanation.

CHAPTER 2

Things That Go Bump in the Night

Many myths have strange monsters in them, such as **trolls** who live under bridges, **ogres** who eat people, and fire-breathing dragons. What exactly is a monster? It's a creature that is not

human and is not a known type of animal.
Sometimes, it is a combination of the two.
Usually, these creatures are very frightening.

New monsters have been reported within
the past hundred years. Some monsters are said
to live in the wild and run from humans. Other
monsters might threaten people who pass their
way. Some monsters walk, and others fly. Water
monsters swim, of course. Do these monsters
really exist? Let's look at some stories so you can
decide for yourself. ⚡

Bigfoot

In 1967, Roger Patterson and Bob Gimlin were
riding horses through the woods in northern
California. Suddenly, the two men saw a large
figure moving nearby. Patterson's horse was so
frightened that it reared up, and its rider tumbled
to the ground. He grabbed his camera and ran
after the figure. The creature moved awkwardly
but quickly. Patterson barely had enough time to
catch the creature on film before it disappeared.

When the photos were processed, they showed a tall, human-like creature covered with hair. It took long strides as it disappeared into the woods. Patterson and Gimlin wondered whether they had seen the creature called "Bigfoot."

The first Bigfoot **sightings** were in the Pacific Northwest in the 1700s. American Indians named the creature *Sasquatch*, or "hairy giant." Almost all reported sightings are alike. It is an ape-like creature between six and eight feet tall that moves very quickly. The creature doesn't seem very interested in humans, but some people believe it might attack if threatened.

Many people thought that the pictures taken by Patterson were proof that Bigfoot exists. Scientists who looked at the pictures, however, couldn't agree on what they showed. Some said they showed Bigfoot. Others said the photos were fakes. Some said the creature was a person in a gorilla suit. They thought that Patterson and Gimlin had staged the whole thing for attention.

Patterson and Gimlin insisted that they hadn't. Patterson died a couple of years after the photos were taken. Years later, even Gimlin wondered if his friend had tricked him.

Some people have worked for years to find solid evidence of Bigfoot. They have found large tracks, reported shadowy sightings, and taken fuzzy pictures. Nothing has helped prove the existence of Bigfoot, though.

One **researcher** has a theory. He believes the description of Bigfoot matches that of a prehistoric animal that was thought to be extinct.

Many pictures of Bigfoot are not clear.

So is Bigfoot a myth or a real creature? We don't know. The best hope for proof would be if scientists could test hair or skin samples. These tests might tell us whether Bigfoot is human or animal. Until someone manages to collect such a sample, though, we won't know for sure whether the monster exists at all.

Water Monsters

For centuries, sailors have reported seeing a wide variety of strange creatures in the sea. Some of these "monsters" were really whales or **squids**. Others were ships or even small islands.

Yet many reports of sea creatures still interest scientists. The deep, dark waters of oceans and lakes can hide many secrets.

Some people have reported seeing creatures that look like giant snakes ranging in length from twenty to forty feet. These creatures are often described as brown or dark gray, sometimes with spots. They are said to move through the water with a rising and falling motion. Because of that, they look like they have humps.

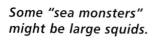

Some "sea monsters" might be large squids.

Other people report seeing water creatures with long necks and small heads. These creatures have rounded bodies with fins or short legs, which make them look a bit like swimming dinosaurs. Most people who report seeing sea monsters say the creatures can stay underwater for a long time.

The Loch Ness Monster

The Loch Ness Monster is the world's most famous water monster. *Loch* is an ancient Scottish word for *lake*. The story of the monster that lives in Scotland's Loch Ness is thousands of years old.

People who lived near Loch Ness in the first century A.D. made drawings showing a strange animal with flippers and a beak. They carved these drawings into large stones. If you visit Scotland today, you can see the carvings on stones that still stand in the Loch Ness area.

In the twentieth century, interest in the Loch Ness Monster grew. In 1933, a couple driving near Loch Ness claimed they saw a giant animal swimming in the lake. More reports followed. People began to travel to Scotland because they wanted to see the monster. A circus offered a reward to anyone who could catch it. Then, a newspaper hired a hunter to track it down. The hunter returned with footprints of the monster, but they were later proven to be fakes.

This photo, taken in 1934, might be the most famous picture of Nessie.

People continued to look for the monster, who was nicknamed "Nessie." They wrote books about it. Universities and scientific groups sent people to study and track it. Sketches based on eyewitness accounts showed a large monster that looked like a dinosaur with flippers.

In the 1970s, a group of people used a **sonar** device to try and find Nessie. This device uses sound to track underwater movement. The group also used an underwater camera. The sonar device recorded a large object moving in the water, and the camera started taking pictures. The photos seemed to show a creature with flippers.

People were excited about the pictures. One scientist thought the pictures proved that Nessie was a kind of water animal that many people thought was extinct. Other scientists argued that it was just a small whale. Some experts even thought the photos were fakes. People still can't agree about what the pictures show.

People still go to Loch Ness hoping for a glimpse of the creature. Maybe someday we'll know the truth about Nessie.

The Gloucester Sea Serpent

Another monster with a long history is the Gloucester Sea Serpent. It was first sighted off the coast of Maine in 1751. Further reports came from the same area. Then, in 1815, someone reported spotting the monster near the city of Gloucester, Massachusetts.

The Gloucester serpent is described as 80 to 140 feet long. It has dark skin with white streaks, and its head is flat like a snake's. A large fin runs down its back, and it has sharp teeth.

Most sightings of the monster took place in the 1800s, though there were a few in the twentieth century. No one has discovered what the monster really is, or if it's a monster at all.

Trunko

One of the strangest sea monsters reported is "Trunko." In 1922, people at a beach in South Africa spotted two whales fighting with an odd creature. The whales seemed to be winning. Eventually, the creature disappeared. The next day, its body washed ashore. This monster was about 47 feet long. It was covered in long, white hair. Strangest of all, the monster didn't have a head! It had a trunk like an elephant instead.

You might think that an actual body would be proof enough that such a creature exists. But Trunko is still a mystery. What happened to the body? Didn't anyone contact the authorities? Were the people who found the body simply too frightened? Or was the whole thing a **hoax**?

◀ *This drawing of "The Great Sea Serpent" was made around 1860.*

The sea is a mysterious place. These sea creatures might be just unusually large fish or snakes. Then again, maybe they really are sea monsters.

Other Strange Monsters

There are other reported monsters that don't fit easily into a group. They aren't humanoid creatures, like Bigfoot, and they're also not water monsters, like Nessie. Two of these strange monsters are "Mothman" and "El Chupacabra." Both were first spotted within the last fifty years. Both apparently can fly.

Mothman is described as a large, frightening gray monster with huge wings. It has glowing red eyes. It was first spotted in 1961 in the Ohio River valley. In 1966, people began to report Mothman sightings near a factory in West Virginia.

El Chupacabra, or "The Goatsucker," is also a flying monster. It has claws, fangs, and red eyes. El Chupacabra **reportedly** sucks the blood from its victims, which can include adult bulls.

El Chupacabra seems ▶
to be a new monster.

There were a few sightings of El Chupacabra in the 1960s, but most reports are from the 1990s. El Chupacabra sightings have been reported in the United States, Mexico, and South America.

The Origin of Monsters

Do these monsters exist? If they don't, how could so many people be wrong about what they've seen? Some scientists say that people who see monsters are just letting their imaginations run wild. However, people who report that they've seen monsters have their own feelings on the subject—they believe!

People today might have more reasons to believe in monsters than ever before. We are surrounded by new technology, new machines, and new chemicals. These things can make our lives easier. Still, many people worry that these things also might be causing problems we don't even know about yet. Could they result in strange, frightening new creatures?

CHAPTER 3

Are We Alone?

In ancient times, people thought that the bright lights they saw in the sky were gods and goddesses. Then, in the early 1900s, people saw flying lights in the sky. Word soon spread that these new lights were actually the first airplanes. When early rockets were launched into space, people looked up and said they saw spaceships from other planets.

Have our imaginations just kept up with technology? Or has technology finally helped us believe that creatures from other planets might exist and even visit our planet? The answer depends on what kind of proof you want.

Science has always needed evidence that explains what things are or how they work. Many scientists say there isn't enough evidence to prove there is intelligent life on any planet except Earth. These scientists want proof, such as a piece of a spaceship or clothing from an **alien**. Without proof, some scientists cannot believe that aliens and **unidentified** flying objects (UFOs) exist.

People who believe aliens do exist say that some scientists just aren't willing to listen to new ideas. Yet there are other scientists who have tried to find proof that aliens exist. These scientists formed a group called SETI (Search for Extraterrestrial Intelligence). SETI uses the latest telescopes and radio technology to watch the skies for signals from other planets. SETI scientists take the possibility of aliens seriously.

What is enough proof for you? Listen to both sides before you decide.

Unidentified Flying Objects (UFOs)

In June 1947, pilot Kenneth Arnold spotted strange, flashing lights while flying near Mount Rainier in Washington. He thought the lights were nine saucer-shaped objects. They flew in a set pattern, like geese flying south for the winter.

Arnold told his story to reporters. Word of the "flying saucer" sighting spread around the country. The United States military forces said that the lights didn't belong to any of their airplanes. Other nations said the same thing.

Some scientists argued that Arnold had seen a meteor shower. Others say he saw lights that were reflecting off some white geese. Some people suspected that the lights belonged to a secret new aircraft. Many people, however, believed that Arnold had seen spaceships flying over Earth.

There have been many reports of similar UFO sightings. People see flashing lights moving in strange patterns. The lights might stop and start suddenly, or move very slowly or very quickly.

In 1980, people in Suffolk, England, saw pulsing lights over a forest. The next day, they found burn marks on the ground. In August 1986, people all over the East Coast of the United States reported strange glowing objects moving across the sky. In 1987, a Japanese Airlines pilot contacted **air traffic controllers** to say he saw the lights of a spaceship behind him. The controllers agreed that there was an unidentified object on their radar. These events were all reported as UFO sightings.

Scientific investigators disagreed, case by case. Research showed that the 1980 lights in England came from a nearby lighthouse. The "burn marks" were scratches made by rabbits. According to some investigators, the objects in the 1986 sightings were a group of Japanese satellites, not UFOs. The Japanese pilot most likely saw the planets Mars and Jupiter reflecting off the moon. The air traffic controllers' strange object was a "bounce-back," or echo of the pilot's own radio signal.

◀ *Are these UFOs real or just a trick of the light?*

Some UFO believers doubt the investigators' reports. They think the government is aware of UFO visits and wants to keep the information from the public. These believers continue to look for proof that UFOs really exist.

Thousands of UFO sightings have been reported over the years. Most have **plausible** explanations. A few don't. What do you think is the truth?

Evidence of Aliens?

People who don't believe in aliens often ask for evidence. People who do believe in them say they have lots of it.

In July 1947, many people saw a flying object crash near Roswell, New Mexico. Mac Brazel found pieces of **wreckage** strewn across his ranch. He brought the pieces to a nearby Air Force base. The officer who saw the pieces believed they were from a flying saucer.

Many believers go to ▶ Roswell, New Mexico, in search of answers.

Brazel contacted reporters and told them about the crash. Newspapers across the United States published the story. The next day, the Air Force said that the story was wrong. They said the wreckage was part of a weather balloon. Many people believe this was the start of a huge government **coverup** of evidence about UFOs and aliens.

One witness thought that the object had been traveling too fast to be a weather balloon. He also said the material found in the wreckage did not seem like anything he had seen on Earth. Other people reported seeing strange writing on the object that did not look like any language they knew.

UFO CRASH SITE

UFO Museum - 114 N. Main - Roswell

There were other reports, too. One Roswell man said that he had seen four small bodies at the Air Force base. A film of an **autopsy** of the bodies was shown on TV in the 1990s. In the 1980s, secret military reports were found that told about the 1947 crash.

Investigators had different answers, though. Experts outside of the United States military forces and the government agreed that the wreckage was indeed a weather balloon. Film experts showed how the autopsy film could have been faked. The military reports found in the 1980s did not match the report-writing style of the 1940s, so they were considered fakes, too.

Is this photo proof of a government coverup?

There has been evidence of aliens other than at Roswell. A man in England took a picture of a shadowy, running figure. The figure is small with a large head. It seems to match people's ideas of what an alien should look like. Some photo experts say the picture is real. Others say, "Fake!"

Many people accept the official explanations. Others wonder if there is a big coverup going on. Believers say aliens are too smart to leave much of a trail, so it's not surprising that there is little evidence.

Kidnapped!

The best evidence of aliens might come from people who have met them. There are many people who claim to have done just that.

In 1961, Betty and Barney Hill were driving home from a vacation. They noticed a bright object in the sky following them. They got out of their car to get a better look. The object was a saucer-shaped aircraft. Barney thought he spotted humanoid figures in its window.

The Hills then drove home, but they later realized they had somehow lost two hours of time. There were also strange marks on their car and on Barney's shoes.

Soon after this, the Hills had nightmares about UFOs and aliens. They dreamed about that night and the missing hours. They agreed to be put under **hypnosis** to find out more. Hypnosis puts people into a state of deep concentration. Sometimes it helps find hidden memories.

Under hypnosis, the Hills said that they remembered being in a spaceship where aliens examined them. The aliens showed the Hills a map of the stars so they could see where the aliens had come from. The Hills came out of hypnosis believing that aliens had abducted them.

Many people tell similar stories. They tell of seeing strange lights outside a window or on the road. Then, they feel as though they can't move.

Later, they realize that periods of time—usually hours—are missing from their life. Hypnosis or dreams later help them remember being in a spaceship and being examined by aliens.

The people who report these stories generally describe the same type of aliens. The aliens are usually about three to four feet tall. They have large heads and large, dark eyes. The aliens might not speak with their mouths, but they seem to communicate with their eyes and their thoughts.

Some people argue that these stories must be true because they are so similar. How could so many people dream or remember the same thing? To many people, this is proof that we are indeed being watched and visited by aliens.

Skeptics react differently. They say hypnosis isn't trustworthy. They warn that sometimes people under hypnosis will not remember things clearly, so they might try to "fill in the blanks."

This photo, taken from the air, shows strange circles made in farmers' fields. Were they made by aliens?

They might come up with ideas that help them believe what they want to believe. They might get some of these ideas from movies and books.

So how can we find out the truth about aliens? Do you need physical evidence to believe, or do the stories convince you? How would you investigate? How would you decide?

CHAPTER 4

This Really Works!

Do you carry a lucky rabbit's foot? Maybe you have a favorite shirt that you wear when you take a test, just for good luck.

These actions are based on superstitions. People believe that superstitions explain why things happen or don't happen. Like myths, superstitions are often invented to calm our fears about the unknown. They tell us that we can avoid bad things or get good things just by following some rules. ⚡

Wish Me Luck!

Take a look at some common superstitions. How many of these have you heard?

- ❀ As you begin a trip, throw an old shoe behind you for good luck.

- If you see a four-leaf clover, pick it for good luck.
- When you visit a newborn baby, kiss the bottoms of its feet to give it good luck.
- When you walk or drive past a cemetery, hold your breath.
- When fishing, throw your first catch back for good luck.

Superstitions have some interesting things in common.

- Most tell you what to do to get good luck or avoid bad luck. By following the rules, you feel you have some control over what happens to you.
- Most give advice that is easy to follow.
- Most refer to common human concerns. People always worry about a new baby's future. Fishermen always look for ways to make the day's catch better.

Do-It-Yourself Superstitions

Athletes often have **personalized** superstitions. Players might think about what they were wearing or doing when they had a good game. They repeat those things in the hopes of having another good game. For example, a soccer player might wear her "lucky" socks for every big game. A basketball player might tug his ear before taking a free throw.

If players convince themselves that their superstitions really work, they actually might play better. After all, they expect to play better because they've done what they think they're supposed to do—they've followed their superstition.

This could be a very lucky baby.

What's Going to Happen?

"Old wives' tales" are similar to superstitions. The big difference is that old wives' tales are **supposedly** based on the wisdom of generations of women. Many old wives' tales are about love and marriage. Some offer home **remedies** for illnesses. Some predict what will happen in the future. Have you heard any of these?

Is this cat predicting rain or just grooming itself?

- A cat washing its face means rain is coming.
- A large number of spiders in the fall means it will be a hard winter.
- Snow on your wedding day means you will be happy and rich.
- A baby born during a new moon will be very strong.

People often fear the unknown, and the future is a big unknown. Before there was any radar or accurate weather equipment, people looked for clues that might help them predict the weather. People are often anxious on their wedding day, so they want indications that everything will be okay. When babies are born, parents look for hints of what the years ahead will bring. People use old wives' tales to help them feel as if they have some control over the future.

Science has shown the foolishness of most superstitions and old wives' tales. Yet many people still follow some superstitions, even if they say they don't really believe them. Why?

It's probably because the advice given is not hard to follow. It's not really much trouble to be careful on Friday the thirteenth. It doesn't take much time to walk around a ladder instead of under it.

Some superstitions and old wives' tales can be rules to help you live well. Just because they sound a little fishy doesn't mean you should always dismiss their advice. How much proof do you need that picking up a penny brings you good luck?

CHAPTER 5

A Friend of a Friend Told Me

Urban legends are like myths. The difference is that urban legends give specific details, such as places, dates, and names. If you say that a story happened to "a friend of a friend," it sounds as if it's true. If you say where and when it happened, then it sounds even more **believable**. Urban legends sound real, but they're usually not.

The phrase *urban legend* first showed up in the 1960s. In the 1950s, cities became bigger, and life seemed to move faster than it had in the past. Traditional fears and concerns weren't as **relevant** to city life, and country superstitions weren't as meaningful to people in cities.

Cities offered people all sorts of new fears and worries, though. New tales sprang up about the dangers of life in modern cities. These stories warned people about bad things that might happen to them or told funny things that had happened to other people. These tales became known as urban legends.

Urban legends are usually passed on by word of mouth. Now they also travel by e-mail. Read the stories that follow. Have you heard any before? If so, did you believe they were true?

Embarrassed

A wealthy man was jogging one morning. He wore an expensive jogging suit and sneakers. Suddenly, a young man in a worn-out T-shirt and shorts bumped into him. After the young man had run by, the wealthy man checked his pockets. His wallet was missing! He sped up, grabbed the young man, and yelled, "Give me the wallet!"

The young man quickly pulled out a wallet, handed it over, and ran away. The wealthy man jogged home. There, he noticed his own wallet sitting on the dining-room table! The wealthy man had just accidentally robbed someone!

A woman stopped at a shop to buy ice cream. As she made her purchase, a movie star walked in. The woman, a huge fan of the star, nearly fainted in surprise. She wanted to look cool in front of the star. She calmly paid for her ice cream and walked out.

◀ *Some people like to be scared by urban legends.*

As she got into her car, she realized she didn't have the ice-cream cone. The clerk must have been so nervous about the movie star that he had forgotten to give it to her. She went back into the store and politely asked the clerk for her cone. The movie star, who was still in the shop, turned to her and smiled. He said, "It's in your purse."

These two urban legends tell about times when a person was really embarrassed. Sometimes the person thought he or she had done something

clever but later realized it was a terrible mistake. People like to hear stories in which other people make mistakes. They feel better about times they did something foolish and were embarrassed.

This kind of urban legend takes many forms. The jogger story is similar to a story about a grandmother who "steals back" her cookies from a young man sitting near her at a train station. She later finds her own cookies tucked away in her purse. She realizes she had stolen the young man's cookies and not the other way around.

The movie-star story changes every few years to use a current popular movie star. This is an important part of urban legends—they keep up with the times.

Urban legends are usually entertaining, but they have a social role, too, like many ancient myths did. They might explain why you should behave one way but not another. Some urban legends show why it doesn't pay to be dishonest or mean. Others show how good behavior will be rewarded.

Just Punishments

On the night before a test, some college students stayed out all night instead of studying. They slept late the next day and missed the test. The group told the teacher that they missed the test because their car had a flat tire. The teacher allowed them to take the test the following day. The students were pleased. They had gotten away with it! Imagine their surprise when they looked at the test. It had only one question: "Which tire was flat?"

A woman bought a cookie in the bakery of a famous department store. It tasted so good that she asked for the recipe. The clerk told her that he couldn't give it to her. She offered to buy it, so the clerk got the recipe. The woman had him charge it to her store credit card.

A month later, the woman received her credit card bill. The recipe had cost $250! She quickly complained to the store, but they told her that was the price of the recipe. They wouldn't give her money back.

To get revenge on the store, the woman sent the recipe by e-mail to everyone she knew. She asked them to pass it on to everyone they knew. Soon the recipe was free to everyone over the Internet. No one would need to buy the recipe—or the cookies—anymore!

Both of these stories are warnings. They tell what can happen to cheaters. In the first story, people cheat and get caught. The second tells about a greedy company and how one woman was able to get revenge. These stories have modern details, but their point is as old as any tale from hundreds of years ago—don't cheat!

Good Deeds

A woman driving across the country pulled off the highway to find a bathroom. The first place she saw was a funeral home. The owners said she could use their bathroom. She noticed that a funeral was going on, but no one was there to honor the dead man. The woman felt sorry for him, so she signed the guest book.

A few weeks later, the woman got a call from a lawyer. The dead man had been very wealthy, but he hadn't made many friends during his life. He had decided that anyone who came to his funeral would **inherit** his money. The woman is now a **billionaire**.

A young man was driving down a highway on a windy, rainy night. He saw a car sitting on the side of the road. The man decided to pull over to see what was wrong.

The car had a flat tire. A husband and wife were struggling to change the tire. The young man changed the tire for them. Because it was dark, it took him a while to realize that the husband was a famous singer. The grateful star asked how he could thank the young man. The man said his wife would be thrilled to get flowers from such a famous person. The singer wrote down the young man's name and address and then drove away.

The next day, the young man's wife received a dozen beautiful roses. The card said they were from the singer. It also said that the singer had paid off all the young couple's bills, including their house!

These two stories have an old message—good people will be rewarded. Because they are urban legends, these stories change to keep up with the times. Years ago, the woman in the first story was said to inherit a few thousand dollars. Now it's billions! Any well-known rich person can replace the famous singer in the second story. With small changes, the stories can be retold for many years.

Oh, Horrors!

A woman spent her vacation at the beach getting a deep, dark tan. She loved the look and wanted to keep it through the winter. She went to a tanning studio. The strong light in the tanning beds helped her stay tanned, but the studio only let her stay in the tanning bed for 15 minutes at a time. She wondered how she could keep her tan when she could only stay a short time.

One day she had an idea. She made an appointment at every tanning studio in or near her town, all for the same day. She spent the whole day at different tanning studios—15 minutes at each studio.

That night, the woman felt very sick. She went to the hospital, where a doctor examined her. Then he asked her what she had done that day. She told him.

"I have bad news," said the doctor. "You spent so much time in the tanning beds that you've broiled your insides!"

A girl loved to swim in the ocean near her home. She spent almost every day there. One day, though, she felt pains in her stomach. The pains wouldn't go away. Her mother took the girl to a hospital. A doctor examined her, and then he immediately operated on her. When she woke up,

the doctor explained the problem. While she was swimming, the girl had swallowed some tiny octopus eggs. The doctor had removed a young octopus from her stomach!

These two stories tell about unusual, horrible things that happen to ordinary people. These legends are products of a nervous world. They warn that danger is everywhere and that bad things can happen in the most unlikely places. They make listeners examine their own behavior so they don't make the same mistakes as the people in the stories.

These stories sound unlikely. Still, you might believe them if the person who told them insisted they were true. After all, they had happened to a friend of a friend. ⚡

CHAPTER 6

I Want to Believe

What does the story of Demeter and Persephone have in common with stories about aliens? Today's myths serve many of the same purposes as those from ancient times. Some ancient myths explained the unknown, such as the sun and the moon and other **celestial** objects. Today's UFO myths also explain odd lights people see in the night sky. Ancient myths explained how disease came into the world. Today's legends suggest what kinds of **mutant** creatures our technology might bring into the world.

People usually stop believing in myths when they find scientific explanations for natural phenomena. Scientists now offer explanations for

Today we know that seasons change as Earth moves around the sun.

most of the phenomena written about in ancient myths. How do we find the explanations behind modern myths?

Scientists prove things by finding evidence. They ask questions. They put together theories and then test them. Myths can be evaluated the same way.

The first step in evaluating whether a tale is a myth is to hear both sides of a story. To make a fair, informed decision you must listen to others and respect their ideas. When you have enough information and have studied others' opinions, then you can put it all together yourself. You might even find the truth.

For some people, the key to the truth is proof. If you ask thoughtful questions about a story, does the story still make sense? When someone gives you evidence, think about it carefully. Does it add up to what the person says? You read about the hunter who produced footprints from the Loch Ness Monster. Those footprints could have proven Nessie's existence. However, **zoologists** showed that they were really just hippopotamus footprints.

Remember that even when myths are proven wrong, some people still believe them. These people might think the scientific explanation is too simple. They might think that someone is trying to hide the truth. Or they might just really want to believe in the myth.

For most of us, myths only exist until we no longer need them. Myths can still be good, entertaining stories, but that's often all they are— stories. Or are they?

Glossary

abducted (ab DUHKT ehd) *verb* Abducted means captured or kidnapped someone.

air traffic controllers (EHR TRAF ihk kuhn TROHL uhrz) *noun* Air traffic controllers are people who use computers to guide airplanes into and out of airports.

alien (AYL ee uhn) *noun* An alien is a creature from another planet.

autopsy (AW tahp see) *noun* An autopsy is the study of a dead body by a doctor to find out the cause of death.

believable (buh LEEV uh buhl) *adjective* Something that is believable can be taken as true or real.

billionaire (bihl yuh NEHR) *noun* A billionaire is a person who possesses at least a billion dollars.

celestial (suh LEHS chuhl) *adjective* Celestial means having to do with the sky or the universe.

compromise (KAHM pruh myz) *noun* A compromise is a way of reaching an agreement in which each side gives something up.

coverup (KUHV uhr uhp) *noun* A coverup is an attempt to keep people from finding out about something.

hoax (HOHKS) *noun* A hoax is a trick or mean joke.

humanoid (HYOO muh noyd) *adjective* Humanoid means having a human-like form or features.

hypnosis (hihp NOH sihs) *noun* Hypnosis is a sleep-like condition in which a person can answer questions and might remember his or her experiences.

inherit (ihn HEHR iht) *verb* To inherit means to receive money or property from someone who has died.

mutant (MYOOT nt) *adjective* A creature that is mutant has changed, sometimes because its environment has changed.

mystifying (MIHS tuh fy ihng) *adjective* Mystifying means confusing or mysterious.

ogres (OH guhrz) *noun* In legends and fairy tales, ogres are giants who eat people.

personalized (PUR suh nuh lyzd) *adjective* Something that is personalized was made especially for you or belongs only to you.

phenomena (fuh NAHM uh nuh) *noun* Phenomena are events or conditions that we can observe in the world around us.

plausible (PLAW zuh buhl) *adjective* Something that is plausible is something that seems true or likely.

relevant (REHL uh vuhnt) *adjective* Relevant means having a connection with something else.

remedies (REHM uh deez) *noun* Remedies are treatments that relieve pain or cure disease.

reportedly (rih PAWRT ihd lee) *adverb* Reportedly means according to reports or accounts.

researcher (REE surch uhr) *noun* A researcher is a person who carefully studies or investigates something.

resided (rih ZYD ehd) *verb* Resided means lived in a certain place.

sightings (SYT ihngz) *noun* Sightings are observations, especially of something unusual.

skeptics (SKEHP tihks) *noun* Skeptics are people who doubt or question a belief.

sonar (SOH nahr) *adjective* A sonar device sends sound waves through water to track movement.

squids (SKWIHDZ) *noun* Squids are marine animals with a long body and ten arms.

starvation (stahr VAY shuhn) *noun* Starvation means death from lack of food.

supposedly (suh POH zihd lee) *adverb* Supposedly means according to what is believed.

trolls (TROHLZ) *noun* Trolls are creatures in folk tales and myths who live in caves, underground, or under bridges.

trustworthy (TRUHST wur thee) *adjective* A trustworthy person is someone who can be trusted.

unidentified (uhn eye DEHN tuh fyd) *adjective* If something is unidentified, people haven't figured out what it is.

urban (UR buhn) *adjective* Urban means having to do with a city or city life.

weighed (WAYD) *verb* To have weighed something means to have considered it.

wreckage (REHK ihj) *noun* Wreckage is the pieces that are left after a vehicle crashes or is damaged.

zoologists (zoh AHL uh jihsts) *noun* Zoologists are scientists who study animals and animal life.

Index